I0472682

THE ANTIDOTE TO EMAIL CHAOS

To my parents,

Rick and Michelle Grace

Published by: Amazon Australia Services, Inc.
Language: English
ASIN: B074PPT195

ISBN: 9781522069270

Contents

Introduction

Early in my career I remember an incident that ignited my curiosity for the art of communication. Most organisations use email as the bedrock for communication because it is a revolutionary communication portal; sending messages instantaneously and accurately. Email is a powerful tool, yet not many of us are taught how to wield it and so this book contains the lessons and secrets I've discovered on how to bring peace and order to the chaos caused by email. If it isn't managed correctly, email has the power to create a chaotic maelstrom in the workplace, like a tornado, leaving a trail of destruction and confusion in its wake. I learnt the first lesson about email that morning – many years ago – as I made a cup of coffee in the staff room:

'Tough morning?'

The voice behind startled me.

I whirled around, alarmed more by the truth spoken than by the interruption. 'How did you know,' I said managing a smile.

The old professor had a white beard and spectacles that balanced precariously on the tip of his nose. He worked in the psychology department down the hall and I had run into him a few times before. He was friendly and always had something interesting to say.

'Just guessing,' he said, 'but also cause I heard you stirring that cup from my office, any harder and you'll create a black hole,' he said as he rubbed a wrinkled hand through his beard.

'Sorry,' I chuckled as my gaze returned to the black liquid. Trust a psychology professor to psycho-analyse my coffee stirring. I wanted to tell him that yes it had been a tough morning, in my head. My imagination had created a myriad of worst case scenarios, devoid from reality because I hadn't even the courage to open my inbox to determine what the reality actually was.

'Just one of those days,' I mumbled.

He didn't give up easily – good psychologists never do – and so he pressed further. 'I've got ten minutes before my next meeting, let's catch up.'

'Sure,' I said, quite happy to procrastinate further. I followed him down the hall and was soon settled on the leather chair in his office. Books bent the shelves and piles of paper had formed turrets on his desk.

'I won't charge you for this session,' he said wryly as he leant back in his chair.

'Thanks,' I said.

He stared at me as he crossed his arms over his waist. His silence forced me to speak.

I took a deep breath then said, 'I've started to feel anxious about checking emails. I didn't check my inbox on Thursday, Friday I was away, and so then the whole weekend I spent worrying about the fact that I hadn't checked my emails. I felt sick coming into work this morning. I still haven't the guts to open my inbox.'

I wanted to finish with a question: is this normal? Instead, I looked down, slightly embarrassed at the ridiculousness of this whole situation.

'Why don't you want to open your inbox?' He asked.

'Because I…I don't know, I guess I'm…well truth is I'm probably scared.'

'Scared of what?'

'I don't know, scared of what people might have said, or what I might need to do, of maybe what I didn't do. It sounds crazy I know but...but is this normal?'

'Well,' he said as he looked at the ceiling as if looking for inspiration. 'I could give you the textbook answer or the real answer. Which would you prefer?'

I stared at him, then said nervously, 'at this stage, any answer will do.'

'Okay,' he said as he stood up and walked to the rows of books. He scanned the middle shelf until he found a worn out book. 'Here,' he said as he handed it to me. 'Read this. It will help. It won't fix everything but it's a small step in the right direction. From what you described to me it is clear you have developed a mild social phobia stemmed within anxiety disorder – that would be the textbook answer – but it's not that simple. The root cause of social phobia is how we communicate with other people, or in other words, the fear of conversation. The fear of dialogue. Language is at the heart of the issue. What's more, speaking and writing are two different languages. Both have their pros and cons and both have their place. So when we send an email we send words right? We send a text-based message?'

I nodded.

'Wrong, we send feelings not words. And if we can send feelings, then we can receive feelings. Email makes this worse because of the time delay. Feelings are sent but are not received immediately, whereas if you're talking face to face with someone, feelings are being transferred and received immediately. You're anxious because you're about to open a world of feelings, and you've made it worse because now you're late to the party. Of course it's going to be overwhelming. Of course you're going to feel anxious, that's perfectly normal.'

'That's a relief.'

'Yes, a relief, but far from sustainable. You have to learn how to manage these feelings, otherwise the confusion will be overwhelming. Also, we as humans have evolved very complex communication patterns. This has only been magnified in this digital age. Emails are flung across organisations without thought, they are flung across the world without a care, it's chaos. It's chaos because we send these feelings without fully understanding how they will be received. Emails are inherently emotional because all communication is emotional. So we must develop emotional mastery, or at the very least, emotional agility.'

'How do I do that?'

He smiled then said, 'with great difficulty. Trying to control feelings is harder than taming the shrew because when you think you've finally got control you will realise you don't. My grandchildren prove this fact. Toddlers who are slaves to their emotions, and it's chaos. They are wild animals running around like they are drunk.' He shook his head as he spoke, but he was smiling. 'I love them of course, but they are a handful.'

'And they'll grow up,' I offered.

'Yes. And you too will grow in this career but it starts with learning to manage your emotions.'

Challenge accepted.

He looked at his watch so I stood up and thanked him.

'Before you go,' he said, as if it was an afterthought, 'take a look at this.' He moved his computer screen slightly toward me as I walked back to see what he wanted to show off.

We both stared at the screen, soaking up the image.

'There's no feeling quite like it,' he said. His screen showed an empty inbox. 'It doesn't last long,' he lamented, 'but it's bliss when my plate is clean. No feelings left in the air here. Unanswered emails bread toxic feelings. And feelings are contagious. And so, I answer emails as quickly as possible."

I left his office with a flicker of hope ignited by curiosity: how can I learn to take control of my inbox, rather than let it dictate how I feel. The balance of this short book will uncover the pieces of this fascinating puzzle, starting with an understanding of what an email actually is…it is always one of three things: either a shout, a cry for help, or a genuine contribution. After these three types of emails are explored we look at how the inbox triggers anxiety. It can become even more overwhelming if it becomes cluttered known as the spring cleaner's dilemma. The heart of the book is on understanding emotions and how they can spread electronically: emotions are contagious, like yawning. Finally, the book finishes with a look at how email has evolved and how we can use our time more wisely in this quest to manage our social capital. The epilogue contains a blueprint for writing an emotionally intelligent email. The point of all this is to answer a simple question that lies at the core of our daily interaction with email: how can we bring peace and order to the chaos caused by email?

One

The three types of email

Emails exist in a pyramid that we tend to
see across all human communication. At the
base, and the largest group, is the shouting.
Talking without listening. People who always
have something to say generally don't stop to
think before they blurt their words out. The
listener is bombarded with a verbal onslaught,
helpless to the shouting. Even worse is when
shouting is done via email. The reader is
bombarded with a non-verbal onslaught.
Furthermore, this shouting doesn't always
have to be negative, sometimes people shout
for attention, or shout because they have
something to sell. The technical term for all
this shouting over email is spam. The term
spam comes from one of Monty Python's
sketches, set in a café where every item on
the menu contains Spam (canned meat):
beans on toast with Spam, sausages with
Spam, milkshakes with Spam, etc. The

excessive amount of Spam, as well as the loud chanting from the patrons (Vikings chanting, 'Spam, Spam, wonderful Spam!') coined the phrase, "spamming the dialogue". According to a Wired business article, MailChimp sends en masse over one billion emails per day. There are a lot of people out there who have something to say, and so to be heard, they shout (with an electronic megaphone) but not a lot of us are listening. If you look at your inbox now, you will probably see that spam (generic or personalised) is the largest group of emails.

The second type of email is a cry for help. Help is the key word here. There are generally three different levels of intensity when using the word help. At the most extreme, is panic. For example, if we left the grill on and our now smoking sausages have ignited the kitchen drapes, and flames are now billowing from the hob, we wouldn't send a panicked email to the fire brigade. In this case we would mostly likely cry (literally) for help over the phone. Very rarely is email used for emergencies (even if it is flagged as important and urgent). The second level of intensity – and the most common type of help – falls under the guise of collaboration. Teamwork makes the dream work and all that. We all need help when working on a team project and most of us send an e-mail (to ask for help) because the phone's too scary. People are generally good at 'flicking' out emails from the safety of their cubicle. You will now begin to see this type of email everyday, not in the subject line of course (people aren't that obvious) but in the content, intent, and tone. As the receiver of this type of email you only really have two options: help them, or ignore them.

The latter option is usually the most popular choice when a cry for help falls under the third category: laziness. If people send you this cry for help, it is usually because they don't want to do said task, so the easiest option is to palm it off (via email) to someone else (you). Email is a great tool for making a problem someone else's problem. It then becomes everyone's problem when the 'Reply All' function is engaged. This type of email is the subtle plague that affects most office communication. It must be avoided at all cost.

Nip this type of email in the proverbial bud, or even better yet, don't ever send one…ever.

Unless you are a spy with the mandate of deliberately sabotaging your organisation. In 1944, the OSS (Office of Strategic Services, the CIA's precursor) created a document entitled the 'Simple Sabotage Field Manual'. The then director of the OSS was William J. Donovan; a man with a chiseled jawline and a steady gaze. He earned the infamous nickname, "Wild Bill" after he refused to remove his insignia as he marched into battle (snipers preferred their targets to be higher-ranked). Although Wild Bill professed annoyance at the name, his wife believed that deep down he loved it. A decorated veteran of World War I, Wild Bill's curriculum vitae boasts (among others) the Medal of Honor, the Distinguished Service Cross, the Silver Star, and the Purple Heart. In 1944, Wild Bill recommended that the 'Simple Sabotage Field Manual' be declassified and distributed to citizens working in enemy states. Almost sixty years later, the CIA declassified it to the public. Some of the sabotage instructions included in the booklet, under Section 11,

'General Interference with Organizations and Production' encouraged saboteurs to:

- Insist on doing everything through "channels"
- Make 'speeches'. Talk as frequently as possible and at great length
- When possible, refer all matters to committees, for "further study and consideration"
- Haggle over precise wordings of communication
- "Misunderstand" orders
- Pester the foreman with unnecessary questions
- Ask endless questions or engage in long correspondence
- Contrive as many interruptions to your work as you can
- Multiply paper work in plausible ways
- Start duplicate files

The last four items are of particular relevance when it comes to email. Not that it is done deliberately, of course, but when our inbox is flooded with long and unnecessary emails, we can easily feel overwhelmed, especially when the majority of the emails we receive are spam, or cries for help.

At the top of the pyramid, and thus the smallest group, is the third category. This is the most important and most under-utilized type of email: a genuine contribution. Very rarely do we see these emails flying around in cyberspace. This can be as simple as a word of encouragement, or as complex as solving someone else's problem. When we craft our emails with this mindset, we can't help but break the cycle of meaningless communication. Making a genuine contribution to others is not only good for the team, but good for the organisation as a whole. The genuine contribution might also manifest itself in a timely response. A small problem can become a bigger problem if not dealt with quickly. For example, a few months ago I received a 'cry for help' email from a person outside my organisation – we were working together on a joint venture – and she was in a different time zone. It was an easy fix and only took me five minutes (and I was awake at 3am anyway because of jetlag) so I did it. Making a timely and genuine contribution to others can greatly improve our professional relationships. The world doesn't need more loud people shouting, whining, and crying for help. The world needs more people who are willing to make a genuine contribution to others. Crafting an email that is a genuine contribution can be as easy as changing your tone, or even as simple as remembering to type "thank-you" at the end.

Two
The inbox trigger

It only takes one email. Just one. And we don't even have to read the email, we might simply see the name of the sender – or notice the subject line – for the floodgates of anxiety to be opened. One email can ignite an immediate negative response: anxiety, frustration, panic, despair, guilt, anger, discomfort, hurt, or inadequacy. As I write this paragraph, I've just noticed one fresh email from a person who shouldn't be emailing me, but alas, it is his cry for help. This is the reason why I try not to have my email open in the background. The problem is that us as the reader, are not always in the mood for helping. If learning to focus is the holy grail of productivity, email notifications is the kryptonite. Now I realise I've juxtaposed two different fables, but don't let that detract from the importance of this simple message: don't underestimate the power of the inbox to alter your mood, to mess with your Zen, to interrupt your groove, to flick the switch, to distract you.

The email inbox is both an essential tool that enhances productivity as well as a portal to other people's problems. It only takes one email to ruin or make your day.

While receiving emails can alter our mood, not checking our emails can be the largest trigger for anxiety. If you have ever taken time off work, or been away unexpectedly for a few days, you would have experienced that feeling of intense anxiety as you get closer to that dreaded moment when you will need to face your inbox. When that moment arrives, even waiting for your email inbox to load can amplify the anxiety. I have often wondered if this has something to do with one's personality, like an inbuilt weakness in our psyche, but I think it is more simple than that. It has a lot to do with our mindset. The anxiety is genuine because we are well aware that of the 49 new emails we receive, 20 of them will require us to do something, or make a decision about something. Our brain is overloaded by this dread of dealing with 20 action items at once. I struggle to make one decision at a time, let alone twenty. And so this spiral of anxiety worsens as we race through the list looking for names and key words, important emails and spam. After the initial assessment we then attempt to try and answer, or justify, why we haven't resolved the problem sooner, or completed that task. This method of checking emails is ineffective and redundant because thankfully there is an alternative.

Before you open your inbox, remind yourself that if you can, you will help. If most emails are indeed a cry for help, you can empower yourself with the belief that you can make a genuine contribution to that person. In other words, replace the anxious emotions with a willingness to help. Furthermore, it helps to add the emotion of curiosity. Become curious about people. Become curious about why people send the types of emails they do. Choose to be curious instead of anxious. This way you will learn more about people as you systematically address each email, dealing with one challenge at a time.

Writing an important email requires a tremendous amount of energy because not only could we be writing to multiple people (i.e. trying to convey meaning that might be interpreted differently by every single one of your recipients) but we also have to convey meaning with non-verbal text. Writing is oftentimes more difficult than talking. Electronic mail is after all, a text-based application. According to researchers from MIT, email is the natural evolution of the written memo. They suggest that the written memo was originally used by firms to communicate with external firms (any internal communication was done face-to-face next to the water-cooler). Any communication with the outside world was very formal. Polite language was imperative. Memos in the mid 19th century were typically characterised by terms such as, 'in response to your esteemed favor' and 'your humble servant' or 'yours faithfully'. As firms grew in size and spread geographically, internal correspondence using the written memo became more important. This served as a type of organisational memory because everything was now captured in written documents. The typewriter, introduced in the 1870s, revolutionised this process. The modern computer, introduced in the 1960s, meant these memos no longer had to be stored on paper. Ever since the first email (sent in 1971), computers have become the most efficient conduit for delivering the written memo but it may never be the most effective; it is far better for an important message to be delivered face-to-face, than by a written memo. But why does the mere thought of having a difficult face-to-face conversation trigger anxiety?

Charles D. Spielberger – a man with a plethora of awards from the American Psychological Association and best known for his work on measuring anxiety – describes anxiety as an "unpleasant emotional state [characterised by] subjective feelings of tension, apprehension, and worry." A research paper entitled "who's afraid of the virtual world?" expands this concept: email anxiety is enhanced because it is so much more than a written memo. Email is now used to create and sustain social relationships. It can also be used to send single messages to large groups of people (a clear association to public speaking). Communicating in this virtual world fuels this tension, apprehension, and worry. Email transcends space and time in a way that the written letter never could. The rules of the game changed as of 1971.

As we continue to play in this ever-evolving game of human communication, remember: emails are simply words. It is our role to first assess our own mindset. A curious and willing-to-help mindset is far more useful than an anxious or apprehensive one. Secondly, we must ask of every email we receive: is this a meaningless shout, a cry for help, or a genuine contribution.

Three

The spring cleaner's dilemma

Two researchers from Carnegie Mellon University conducted a study on email inbox overload. They surveyed five hundred white-collar workers asking them questions about how they used emails at work. While they found obvious support for the fact that higher volumes of emails had a direct impact on higher levels of stress, they did discover an interesting and counter-intuitive fact. Not all email management tactics reduce the feeling of anxiety. One particular tactic inadvertently amplified anxiety: filing emails into folders and sub-folders. Creating large hierarchies of folders, while logical, places a burden on our sub-conscious. The burden is light at the start but grows quickly. The hassle to always be on-top of the filing and sorting becomes more demanding as you receive more and more emails. Filing emails is meant to bring order but instead it brings chaos as you wrestle with the never-ending influx. Intense anxiety is amplified by trying to remember where you stored that one important email, whether you stored it at all, or perhaps deleted it by mistake.

This psychological paradox is known as the spring cleaner's dilemma. Steve Whittaker and Candace Sidner suggest that email is not being used for what it was originally designed for: communication. Instead it is being used for task management, personal archiving and filing. They suggest the spring cleaner's dilemma applies to email storage. Some people treat their email inbox the same way they treat their garage. Every three months they begin the grandiose 'spring clean'. It may take three days but it feels liberating once it is done. The dilemma is as follows: even though energy is saved by not constantly worrying about storing and filing, energy is wasted by the impending dread of doing the 'spring clean'. At the back of the spring cleaner's mind is this awareness that one day they will need to revisit all these old and long forgotten emails. Worrying about all these emails puts a subconscious drain on our energy reserves that would better be used for actually doing the work we are paid to do.

The solution to the spring cleaner's dilemma is simple. Deal with each email immediately, and deal with it once. I once read that Lance Armstrong never had a to-do list because he just did it immediately, but maybe this was just what he said on a Nike ad. Nevertheless, to-do lists weigh us down and unless we start doing, the list will keep growing. So, when it comes to the email inbox, you should inevitably be doing one of three things to every email: replying, archiving, or deleting. While this rule is simple in theory, even I find myself reading an email then doing none of those three options and leaving it to stew in the inbox. Usually this is because I don't have the mental aptitude to complete the task immediately or because I need more time to figure out the answer before I reply. But, if we delay the essential tasks of replying, archiving, or deleting, then we let procrastination seep in. We come dangerously close to unintentionally inviting anxiety in; a houseguest that always overstays its welcome. Dealing with each email immediately is a discipline that might seem tedious at the time but it saves us time in the long run.

In summary, learn to keep your space clutter-free. Also, don't waste time and energy over-filing emails. In fact you only really have to worry about three folders: inbox, archives, and trash. With most good email platforms, the archive button is next to the delete button. These two buttons are a God-send. With the GMaill app you can swipe left to archive immediately. Archive an important email once you have dealt with it. Don't worry about not being able to find it later because chances are you probably won't ever need to find it again, and if you do need to find it again, most email platforms have a good search function. If it is that important, you will find it. Archiving an email removes it from your plate. On the other hand, the 'Delete' button removes it from the plate forever. If it is generic spam, or if the company behind it has badgered you enough, scroll to the bottom and hit 'unsubscribe' (look for the small writing). And please don't be afraid to unsubscribe – you're not going to miss out. There is enough information out in the world wide web to find if you really want to. Unsolicited information will fill your plate in an instant, if you let it. So, unsubscribe from as many lists as you can. If you don't know which lists to unsubscribe from ask yourself: "does this bring me joy?" This is the same question Marie Kondo encourages us to ask about each of our belongings. If it doesn't bring us joy, then why keep it. Applying this same principle to managing our inbox, if a regular newsletter is causing you frustration, unsubscribe. Clear the clutter from your inbox and do this everyday, not every Spring.

Four

Understanding emotions (part one): the transference of contagious emotions

We like to think of ourselves as emotionally intelligent – but unfortunately all of us have an inbuilt flaw: emotion is contagious and we can be infected unconsciously. In the fascinating book Emotional Contagion, Elaine Hatfield tells the story of how for years she was infected unconsciously with anxiety from another colleague. Every time she met with James (not his real name) she came away feeling as if she had said something stupid or had bored him. But during one particularly heated discussion she realised that she was only paying attention to how she felt; her own feelings instead of his. So she stopped focusing on herself and began to analyse his state. It occurred to her that even though James was successful, popular and intimidating, at the core he was acutely anxious. The signs were subtle: brief twitches, a slightly elevated pitch in his voice, shifting weight from one foot to another. The next time they met, instead of worrying about her own emotional state, she focused on sending reassuring signals to her anxious friend. It worked; they both settled down.

This incident shows how sensitive we are to the pervasiveness of others' emotions. Even though we may think we are emotionally intelligent, when it comes to contagious emotions that we pick up unconsciously, we aren't immune. The same way we pick up the flu or a virus, we can catch a strong dose of sadness from those around us. On the other hand, this can be positive because some people can infect us with their enthusiasm. Arne Öhman, a psychologist at the Karolinska Institute, responsible for deciding the recipients of the Nobel Prize in physiology or medicine, has developed countless experiments focusing on the influence of emotion, especially fear. After all, fear can be useful. In a dangerous environment, fear can help keep us alive. Then problem comes when we think we are in a dangerous environment, but we aren't.

Scientists have identified four main types of fear: (1) fear of death, (2) fear of animals, (3) agoraphobic fears – distress caused by confined spaces, or large crowds, or places where there is no escape such as bridges, tunnels or trains – and (4) social fear. Social fear manifests in social interactions where there is a fear of criticism, conflict, rejection, or aggression. Social fear is a genuine fear, albeit not always useful. Arne Öhman's experiments measured people's heart rate, skin temperature, and various other physiological responses while showing different images. Flowers, buildings, as well as pictures of snakes and angry faces. But the images of the snakes and angry faces were disguised. They were only shown for 30 milliseconds before the pictures of flowers and buildings reappeared. In other words, the snake was too quick to see. The results were fascinating – even though the subjects couldn't see the fearful images, they felt them. And their body was quick at preparing to defend themselves. Their heart rates went up and they showed increased skin conductance responses. It was as if their body was preparing for fight or flight without asking for the conscious brain's permission.

Joseph LeDoux, director of the Emotional Brain Institute at New York University, says "our brain is basically an unconscious machine." This machine is capable of processing much more than we give it credit for, as exemplified in fear of a threat to our safety: the speed of emotional processing seems to bypass conscious thought. This has been described as an "inescapable emotional response" or an "automatic mechanism" independent of cognition. In other words, our intuition. Arne Öhman believes that a considerable amount of emotional activity is constantly (and automatically) monitoring the world around us, independent from our conscious thought. But should we trust this computer? Should we trust this emotional activity? Should we trust our gut feeling? Or perhaps an even better question is: how much of an influence do our emotions have on our every day decisions? And if they do have an influence, can they be transferred via email?

The answer is found in the work of Antonio Damasio, a Portuguese born professor of Neuroscience who speaks with a calm demeanour and wears circular spectacles in the same vintage style as John Lennon. He has accumulated a wealth of knowledge on the subject of consciousness and developed an influential theory known as the Somatic Marker hypothesis. It is based on the remarkable survival story of Phineas Gage who was working on Vermont's railroad expansion in 1848. An accident involving dynamite sent an iron rod through Gage's left cheek and out through the top of his skull. The strike seemed deadly, but he survived. Months later, the attending physician was recorded as saying, 'I dressed him, God healed him.'

Even though Gage survived, he walked away with a new personality: a destructive demeanour that was not consistent with the successful (and friendly) Gage prior to the accident. He was no longer himself, despite his miraculous survival. He began to make unreasonable decisions that made him unemployable, he tried working on horse farms but was prone to quit or was fired for lack of effort. He died from an epileptic convulsion thirteen years after the accident, at the age of thirty-eight.

Today, his skull and the tamping iron that caused the injury are on permanent display at the Warren Anatomical Museum of Harvard University. Gage's story suggests there is a section of the brain that is responsible for deciphering emotion and social interaction. Just as there are certain sections that are responsible for language and motor skills. Our ability to function in social settings, as well as our ability to take pride in our work, act ethically, obey social conventions, and write emails, all seem to occur in the section of our brain known as the Ventromedial region in the pre-frontal cortex. Like Gage, many patients who have suffered damage in this area seem to be hindered in their daily decision making and social interaction. Their lives seem to fall apart because of poor decisions. Damasio's conclusion: decisions were no longer informed by emotion. Impaired decision making was the result of the legion that disrupted neural pathways between the pre-frontal cortex and the amygdala, the region of the brain responsible for decision-making and emotional responses. Emotional feedback plays a crucial role in decision-making.

Therefore, if some emotions are contagious and emotions play a crucial role in our decision-making, the people we surround ourselves with do have an influence on us. The emotional state of our colleague, teammate, friend, or family member does affect us. If emotions can be transferred from one person to another, it follows that emotions can be transferred via email.

Arm's length electronic management.
Email is no doubt a versatile tool. It has even enabled a unique management style known as arm's length electronic management. The original saying, at arm's length, originally comes from antiquity where a cubit was measured using the forearm's length: from the elbow to the tip of the middle finger. On average, 18 inches became the standard length of a cubit; an arm's length. The lawyers commandeered this term in the late 19th century to ensure parties to a transaction

remained independent. An arm's length transaction meant both parties were independent and thus less likely to collude. An arm's length distance away from another person is a safe distance. Sitting behind a computer screen and emailing people from the safety of your cubicle is even safer. And thus the arm's length manager was born. Email allows them to achieve two main goals: first, by constantly firing off emails they look busy. Secondly, they can create a paper-trail of responsibility so that if (and when) something goes wrong they can always rebut with, 'but I sent you an email...'

Eric Garton, a man with an MBA from Harvard, asked this great question: "what if companies managed people as carefully as they managed money?" Financial capital seems to always be considered of higher value than human capital. People can be replaced, money can't. Well, that was the mantra of the industrial age – constantly monitor the money, in case we lose it – but more and more companies are waking up to the fact that people are their 'scarcest (and most valuable) resource'. One principle that is often forgotten by managers is: the finances needs to be micro-managed, but not the people. People need to be lead. People need to be guided. Leadership requires a certain amount of emotional agility because not all people are the same. And as diverse as people are, there is an equal need for diversity in management styles. Different strokes for different folks.

A few years ago I attended a marketing seminar and one of the keynote speakers used the following anecdote to start his talk. He was the manager of a large team and was in a hurry to pack up one Friday evening: his well-earnt four weeks of annual leave was about to begin. The last thing on his to do list was to set his out-of-office reply. In his haste, and because of his slightly dyslexic tendencies (only when he's stressed, he assured us) he set the email message as: "I will be away on anal leave and returning on the 15th January". He realised who his true friends were on Monday morning when he started to receive the phone calls. Email is a powerful tool, and the source of its power is words. Words are worlds. Words carry meaning. Words carry weight. Misspelt words can be the source of embarrassment. Incorrect grammar can be frustrating.

Managers who embrace the arm's length electronic management style should realise that it is ineffective in the long run. They will only add to the electronic maelstrom. The words they send have power. A careless word, or an unnecessary request to an employee can begin a ripple effect of wasted time and pointless communication.

Five

Understanding emotions (part two): that angry email, write it but don't send it

Early in my career I was served a great injustice, or so I wholeheartedly believed at the time, and so I responded by writing an angry email. It was lengthy. It was also true, at least from my side of the injustice. I finished writing it, and then with great pride I sent it to the four people involved. **In the blink of an eye I had done something irreparable**, and it is still to this day one of the few regrets I live with. It went out to the four recipients and no-one replied. Only two of the four phoned me the next day and after a lengthy (old-fashioned) conversation I started to feel a little better. **Even though it felt great to vent**, I should never have sent it, but in the folly of youth I probably wouldn't have listened to anyone advising me not to hit send. My rage consumed me. I had something that needed to be said, and I had the means by which to do it: an electronic megaphone at my disposal. In all honesty, it was an act of rage, as much as it was an act of cowardice and fear. **I wasn't brave enough to pick up the phone**, or meet them in person to face the confrontation. I sent an angry email, and ten years later I'm still living with that regret. But then what good is a mistake if you can't learn from it.

Cal Newport writes in a Harvard Business Review article that a contributing factor to this epidemic is the low marginal cost of "shooting off" an email. It's too easy to send an email. It doesn't cost anything. Instead of carefully crafting a tactful response or carefully thinking of who needs what information and at what time, we flick off emails like a magician with a shiny new deck of cards. If you work in a large team, this unstructured type of communication inevitably spirals out of control as messages are sent back and forth in an effort to gain clarification. The Reply All function is engaged and soon there is a flood of emails whirling around the office. It's too easy to send an email to everyone with information that no-one needs.

That angry email I sent was a combination of the first two categories. It was a shout. But more than that, it was a cry for help. My feelings were hurt, and as a child would do, I expressed this hurt, with virtual kicking and screaming and a banging of my fists on the desk. Looking back on it, I am grateful for the grace and patience shown by those two colleagues who responded. Getting angry wasn't my mistake though. No: anger can be useful. My mistake was in how I chose to channel that anger. My mistake was in how I reacted: I indulged in my anger.

According to a group of psychologists at Sheffield University, indulgence is one of four ways in which humans process emotion. This is usually done automatically. It is very easy to concentrate on the emotion; fully immersing ourselves in the "wave of [insert emotion here]". For example, the wave of anxiety, or the blind rage, or the overwhelming despair. On the other hand, the second way to deal with an emotion is to avoid it. We try and distract ourselves from the usual painful emotion. For example, typically we don't like to feel embarrassed or feel rejection, so we might avoid asking a question in a public forum. We bite our tongue, so as to avoid feeling that particular emotion.

The third and most dangerous way to deal with an emotion is to suppress it. We often hide our true feelings; burying them deep in our psyche. We learn to become great at disguising our true feelings. People often try to disassociate themselves from their feelings. In a psychological study conducted at the Rosalind Franklin University of Medicine and Science, the researchers measuring this construct told participants to suppress the feeling and hide any evidence that they are actually experiencing the emotion. In other words, to do their best to put it out of their mind. But it is much harder to remove it from the depths of your sub-conscious mind; especially if it has grown roots.

The fourth way to deal with an emotion is to reappraise it. Reassessing an emotional signal can be of great value. Oscar Wilde said, 'I don't want to be at the mercy of my emotions, I want to use them, to enjoy them.'

Instead of seeing emotions as negative and chaotic, far better to reappraise the real meaning that the emotion is trying to deliver. That old adage: "fear is not real, danger is, but fear is simply the story we tell ourselves about the danger." If we trivialize our emotions, ignore them, or suppress them, we will never learn from them. I learnt a great deal from that one angry email. Now, whenever I am served an injustice, I write the angry email, crafting it with great gusto. After I complete it, on multiple occasions I have almost sent it. It is so very tempting to send it. But I have never regretted my decision to refrain. Be brave. Don't fire off angry emails from the safety of your cubicle, instead appreciate the emotions you are feeling and learn from them, then resolve the issue face-to-face. Don't use email to vent; write the angry email, but don't send it.

We send feelings, not words.

At a seminar I attended recently I tried to implement some of Nick Morgan's Power Cues. The subtitle of his book is: the subtle science of leading groups, persuading others and maximizing your personal impact. I focused on my posture (shoulders back when entering the room), I smiled (at no-one in particular), I did my best to conquer distractions so as to appear more charismatic (with little success), and I tried to tune into the other 450 strong delegate's unconscious signals (a task that is harder than it sounds). I learnt more from this experience, more than the actual seminar. This was the lesson: if face-to-face interaction with others has all these subtle cues, communicating via email must also have subtle cues.

A professor I talked to early in my career was convinced that we all needed to use more emoticons when writing emails. A picture speaks a thousand words. And so perhaps, when we are crafting our emails, we are adding subtle cues in our tone. Chaos is caused when we are not aware of these subtle cues we are sending, or even worse, our cues are misinterpreted. People often fail to read between the lines because they are reading too quickly. So if people misread words, then they will also misjudge tones.

Non-verbal tones are even subtler than words, and thus more likely to be misinterpreted. Emoticons help to soften the blow by adding some hint as to the emotional undertone. That being said, you can't really fill the body of professional memo with smiley faces :) but you can take the time to think about what you need to say, and how best to say it, as well as re-read it before sending.

Six

The blueprint for

the digital age

Claude Shannon was born in Michigan four years after the Titanic's maiden voyage across the Atlantic. Twenty seven later, in 1943, he began working with Alan Turing on data decryption and code breaking. Post World War II, in 1948, he published the blueprint that would revolutionise how we understand communication. He wrote the blueprint for digital information architecture. Every time we send an email, across the Atlantic or to any part of the world, we send information using his algorithms. He came up with the formula for encoding a message into a binary digit, error free. Using the Shannon limit, an email message is guaranteed to be sent anywhere without every losing any information (so you can't blame that missing full stop on technology). For example, if you've ever made a long-distance phone call, or made a call in a secluded area with bad reception, you would have experienced the frustration of disruption. The message is garbled. Radio signals also have this weakness; if not tuned to the exact frequency, communication is disrupted. Emails don't – nor will they ever – have this problem because messages are sent at a much slower and safer speed than sound waves. The blueprint that has built the electronic-mail-monolith is rock solid, thanks to the pioneering work of Claude Shannon.

Without getting into more complex concepts such as source coding, message entropy, and spread spectrums, we will focus on the one simple factor, that if understood, would revolutionise how we understand email, and therefore, how we send emails: the holy grail is reliable communication in a noisy world. Everything we thought about communication changed on one October afternoon in 1957. In the middle of a desert in southern Kazakhstan, the Russians launched Sputnik from the Baikonur Cosmodrome. Sputnik was in essence a portable radio tower that looked like a bowling ball with spikes. It weighed only 83 kilograms but could orbit the entire earth in 96 minutes. While it only lasted for 3 months, it did begin the space race, and trigger the Sputnik Crisis. Coined by President Eisenhower, the Sputnik Crisis was a term that brought fear to the American people on a scale similar to that felt by the attack on Pearl Harbour. Not to be outdone, the American's own Explorer 1 communication satellite, weighing only 13 kilograms, was launched four months after Sputnik. NASA was born and men would be leaping around on the moon 12 years later.

Why all the military and political interest in Sputnik? It all came down to communication. During a time of war, superior communication techniques (internally) and superior date encryption techniques (externally) meant victory. Reliable communication in noisy environments is a real problem. Finding the blueprint for a solution was the modern Holy Grail. Today, when we choose email to communicate, many of us are unaware of what goes on behind the scenes. After you hit send, it is unpacked by servers, scanned for viruses, duplicated to make backups, then sent across thousands of miles of cable often in the wrong direction: an email from America to London can go via Japan before it finally arrives at the intended inbox. Reliable communication in a global environment is the reason email will never be eliminated. Email achieves this goal brilliantly, and seamlessly, error free.

That being said, it means nothing because even though we have all the technology in place, all the processes in place, and all the infrastructure in place we send garbled messages. Many of us have not been taught how to communicate effectively with the written word (if you would like to learn, start with Strunk and White's, the Elements of Style). Computer scientists work tirelessly to reduce the noise in communication channels, yet we send noise without thinking. We know this because there is nothing more refreshing than receiving a clear, simple, and concise email. A concisely written message that provides the reader with confidence because of the clarity can be truly refreshing. Our messages are being sent with electronic intelligence at super-sonic speeds but they aren't being written with emotional intelligence: a blueprint for writing emotionally intelligent emails is contained in the Epilogue.

Seven

Using time wisely: living in our inbox, or wasting time in our inbox

There are many theories on how best to spend our time on email. Some have scientific backing, but most have pseudo-scientific underpinnings. There are six main theories. I came up with the last theory so keep in mind that even though it hasn't gone through rigorous scientific examination and might be accused of being pseudoscience, it is a result of my own time spent analysing the rules of email, how time is distorted, and how best to manage my own inbox. All the theories though have their strengths and weaknesses, so it is up to you to decide which works best for you, in your chosen profession.

The first theory suggests that you should only check your inbox once a day. Preferably at the beginning of the day. Furthermore, it is important to give yourself a maximum allotted time of one hour. A good idea in theory because you can then spend the rest of your day doing 'real work'. Joshua Milburn, the minimalist, suggests that we should check email like a minimalist. He checks it once a day, and some days he doesn't check it all. This laissez-faire approach, while appealing, has its limitations.

Another theory that helps to combat some of these limitations, suggests it is much better to have brief check-in times. This fosters a more structured love/hate relationship with our inbox. Alexandra Samuel suggests, we all need to work smarter with our inbox. She says to set an email budget. And be frugal. Allocate [x amount] of total time each day. Then divide it up. Scatter these five to ten minute intervals around your daily planner so you can then periodically check in; like you are on parole. One commentator referred to this as scheduling 'purging' times. It's the word purging that arrests me. Such a strong word. As if we needed to purge our inbox from unsolicited and invited intruders at five to ten minute intervals; as if we need to have ongoing interventions with our inbox.

The theory continues: while 'checked-in', focus only on the emails that matter, ignore the rest, time is precious. While 'checked-out' focus on doing 'real work'. But while this theory has merit, it too has limitations. The day is never as ordered and neat as one would hope when buying a brand new Kikki-K daily planner. Days are generally chaotic, and hence difficult to plan.

A theory to remove yourself completely from inbox chaos is "automation". Set a 24/7 out-of-office message explaining that you are permanently busy doing other things and you will do your best to respond at a time that is more convenient, and that time may be never. While this might be convenient for the receiver because an automatic expectation has been sent, it is very inconvenient for the sender: they have just flicked off an email and one comes back immediately. Like a game of virtual hot-potato. I had a friend who had set up this type of automatic 24/7 message system. It said something along the lines of: "thank-you for your email. It is important to me. Generally I respond to all emails in 1-4 days. Kind regards…" I stopped emailing her because it annoyed me that she was automatically filling up my email inbox with these generic messages. It also became very repetitive as I received this same email response every time! Lines of communication can easily be clogged. Our goal should not be to add to the sludge, nor should it be to frustrate the sender. Automatic responses are like unsolicited advertisements; they are and always will be frustrating.

So forget about automation and forget about checking your inbox like a minimalist, one theory says to forget it all together. Eliminate email. Cal Newport suggests we should replace the chaos of email with structured workflow. Replace email with other tools: the telephone, Slack, MSN instant messenger, Facebook messenger, Yammer, Twitter, ravens, smoke signals, etc. While good in theory, eliminating email would be a step-backward for mankind. It is also a pipe-dream. Email is too popular and too useful for us to ever get rid of. Email works. We just have not quite figured out how to make it work well. Email connects us and if we eradicate it from our lives we will only seek out other ways to connect.

So, assuming we all agree that email can stay, what is the best and wisest way to use our precious time. The most scientifically rigorous study I have found contravenes conventional wisdom. Scientists from Carnegie Mellon University found that intermittent checking at five to ten minute intervals, or checking emails once a day, actually caused more stress. People felt more overwhelmed because they had to deal with bulk demands all at once. They found that dealing with emails as they come in, whenever a new message arrives, helps us to feel more in control and more connected. We can also help people in a timely manner by responding to easy queries immediately. The downside of this theory, we begin to live in our inbox. We become addicted to constantly being connected to the digital landscape. Between office hours is understandable, but this can have dire consequences if we bring our inbox home with us. Work emails infiltrate our personal lives through the mobile phone.

Our inbox can set up shop within the walls of our own home, if we let it.

The solution: take control of your inbox. Don't let it control you. The inbox should be your servant not your master. If we treat the inbox like a ball and chain, whereby we have to check it at 11:15 everyday, or we constantly need to 'purge' it, or we can only ever check it once a day, at the end of every day, we will exhaust ourselves. Instead, understand the inbox for what it really is: a portal that allows us to connect with others. A portal that allows us to provide genuine contribution to the lives of others. So to do this in the most efficient and effective way possible, try applying the following method.

STEP ONE. Before you open your inbox, remind yourself that most emails sent (by humans) will be cries for help and the best way to respond to this is with a genuine contribution. Every email we send should add value to other people, every email should be a genuine contribution to another. However, we can't always do this, sometimes we are the ones who need help. We all need help at times, so when you do need to send a 'cry for help' remember to ask politely. Hint: the magic phrase to use at the start is – I have a favour to ask... Also, remember that when you ask for help, what you are really demanding is people's time. And people are very protective of their time, so ask politely. But be prepared to receive impolite cries for help.

STEP TWO. Get ready to open your inbox. Now, if you feel a wave of anxiety every time you even think of checking you inbox, retrain that neurological pathway. This requires effort and repetition. Remind yourself that the inbox is your slave, not your master, and you will use it to help others if you can, and if you cannot, you can help point them in the right direction. Replace the anxious mindset with a curious and helpful mindset.

STEP THREE. Once you are in the correct headspace, Open your inbox. Ignore the bold (49) new emails signal and direct your focus by scrolling down to the bottom of the page. Start at the bottom. Oldest email first. Focus on one email at a time. For each email: reply to it, archive it, or delete it.

STEP FOUR. Commit to clearing the clutter and aim for an empty inbox, no matter how long it takes. Work hard to make this happen, it becomes easier as you gain momentum. And the result of your labour will be a liberating feeling that money cannot buy. Microsoft Outlook has a message that appears when you achieve this Holy Grail – you're all caught up. The Gmail app shows a picture of a person relaxing on a beach chair at sunset. An empty inbox brings with it peace of mind.

STEP FIVE. Once you have an empty inbox, you are now free. Free to focus on 'real work'. Free to focus on your agenda, not the demands of others. Free for a moment until that next email comes in. For this reason I close my inbox. I don't want it tormenting me in the background. I also turn off email notifications, both on my phone and computer. I don't need the distraction of an alert to let me know that I have an email. If I'm not in my inbox, I'm generally focusing on other work, and thus in that mindset, not in the mindset for helping people. So when you are finished your other tasks (the real work) and are ready to communicate with others again (the hard work), go back to step one. Repeat.

Epilogue
The blueprint for writing an emotionally intelligent email

The email communication channel has evolved immensely since the first email was sent in 1971. Try to think of email as a network of roads. Roads are busy, noisy, there is often traffic congestion, and occasionally people drive the wrong way. Email is an information highway; help reduce the congestion by using the following blueprint.

1. **Keep it simple.** According to Strunk and White: omit needless words. A clear and concise email is the goal. If you finish writing the message and it is longer than seven lines, consider not sending it and have that exact some conversation over the phone instead. All messages need to be decoded: try to make the task as easy as possible.

2. **Build rapport with the reader.**

    There are two easy ways to do this. (1) Be polite. Use, 'I have a favour to ask' instead of 'do this by...'. Another magic word is 'yet' instead of 'but'. There's also magic in the word 'because' as it brings immediate clarification. Thank-you, please, and sorry also go a long way to help build mutual respect and amicability. (2) Mirror their style. If you are replying to an email, look at how they started and finished. Mirror that style. Write in their language. If they used one sentence: use one sentence in your reply. If they composed a lengthy paragraph: reply with the same. If they ended with Kind regards: do the same. Try not to make it too obvious though and don't compromise your own style or integrity to mirror someone else. However, this principle is used in face-to-face interaction by people who naturally mirror the sub-conscious movements of each other. If it can work with our body language, then it can work with our written language. Remember, we send feelings not words.

3.   **Avoid Clutter.** If there have been multiple conversations, and multiple threads, a lot of superfluous information can build up at the bottom of the email (previous conversations, repeated signature blocks, etc.,) Delete it all by hitting CTRL + A, then Delete. You can then compose in the blank space.

4.   **Write as you would speak**. Write in a way that comes naturally to you because in essence you are having a conversation. This will help capture the correct tone.

5.   **Avoid firing off emails.** Re-read the finished email before sending, even if it is one sentence. First, to pick up spelling and grammar mistakes. Secondly, to read between the lines

because the person receiving it will be doing exactly that.

6. **Don't' dilly-dally.** Do not, under any circumstances send a 'delay-email'. This tactic is a subversive tactic and is usually a disguise for laziness. An email reply with 'I will try and get this to by Thursday' wastes everyone's time because the question remains unanswered. And now there are more emails to deal with as messages are sent back and forth. Write meaningful emails that provide a genuine contribution, not 'delay-emails'. As a side note, the etymology of the phrase "dilly-dally" comes from the old French meaning dille to chat idly. And the Anglo-French dalier meaning to amuse oneself. Therefore don't dilly-dally with emails, chatting idly as you amuse yourself sending frivolous electronic messages…

7. **Emails have weight; use them wisely.** The emails you send everyday, day-in and day-out, become an extension of who you are, and how you are perceived in the corporate world. Email, as with any type of communication, it is all about substance and style: what you say and how you say it. Both are equally important. Develop your own style because words have weight, and ensure your communication has substance; it is your word after all.

Digital or not, it is your word. And your words have the power to create chaotic electronic maelstroms or to bring peace and order.

Endnotes

Chapter one
1. The article from Klint Finley goes on to talk about batch sending to avoid spam filters. Spamming really is both an art and a science...Finley, K., (2016). Mailchimp sends a billion emails a day. That's the easy part. Wired. Retrieved from https://www.wired.com/2016/07/mailchimp-sends-billion-emails-day-thats-easy-part. Retrieved on 27 July 2017.

2. The CIA released the 'Simple Sabotage Field Manual' to the public as an unclassified document on 2012. The full manual can be accessed from https://www.cia.gov/news-information/featured-story-archive/2012-featured-story-archive/simple-sabotage.html.

Chapter two
1. Dabbish, L. A., & Kraut, R. E. (2006, November). Email overload at work: an analysis of factors associated with email strain. In Proceedings of the 2006 20th anniversary conference on Computer supported cooperative work (pp. 431-440). ACM.

2. The natural evolution of the written memo Yates, J., & Orlikowski, W. J. (1992). Genres of organizational communication: A

structurational approach to studying communication and media. Academy of management review, 17(2), 299-326.

3. Spielberger, C. D. (1972). Conceptual and methodological issues in anxiety research. Anxiety: Current trends in theory and research, 2, 481-493.

4. Brown, S. A., Fuller, R. M., & Vician, C. (2004). Who's afraid of the virtual world? Anxiety and computer-mediated communication. Journal of the Association for Information Systems, 5(2), 2.

5. Whittaker, S., & Sidner, C. (1996, April). Email overload: exploring personal information management of email. In Proceedings of the SIGCHI conference on Human factors in computing systems (pp. 276-283). ACM.

Chapter three
1. Kondo, M. (2014). The Life-Changing Magic of Tidying Up: The Japanese Art of Decluttering and Organizing. Ten Speed Press.

Chapter four

1. Hatfield, E., Cacioppo, J. T, & Rapson, R. L. (1994). Emotional Contagion. New York: Cambridge University Press.

2. Öhman, A., Flykt, A., & Esteves, F. (2001). Emotion drives attention: detecting the snake in the grass. Journal of experimental psychology: general, 130(3), 466.

3. Scientists have identified four types of fear – see: Arrindell, W. A., Pickersgill, M. J., Merckelbach, H., Ardon, A. M., & Cornet, F. C. (1991). Phobic dimensions: III. Factor analytic approaches to the study of common phobic fears; an updated review of findings obtained with adult subjects. Advances in behaviour research and therapy, 13(2), 73-130.

4. Joseph LeDoux. Retrieved from https://www.youtube.com/watch?v= dGaRPQtAlkM. Retrieved on 28 July 2017.

5. Ohman, A., & Wiens, S. (2001). To think and to feel: nonconscious emotional activation and consciousness. Ed. Kaszniak, A. Emotions, Qualia and Consciousness. World Scientific, Singapore, 235-246.

6. Damasio, A. R. (2006). Descartes' Error. New York: Random House.

7. Garton, E. (2017) What if companies managed people as carefully as they manage

money? Harvard Business Review. Retrieved from https://hbr.org/2017/05/what-if-companies-managed-people-as-carefully-as-they-manage-money. Retrieved on 28 July 2017.

Chapter five
1. Newport, C. (2016). A modest proposal: eliminate email. Retrieved from https://hbr.org/2016/02/a-modest-proposal-eliminate-email. Retrieved on 27 July 2017.

2. Webb, T. L., Miles, E., & Sheeran, P. (2012). Dealing with feeling: a meta-analysis of the effectiveness of strategies derived from the process model of emotion regulation. Psychological bulletin, 138(4), 775.

3. Quartana, P. J., & Burns, J. W. (2007). Painful consequences of anger suppression. Emotion, 7(2), 400.

4. Oscar Wilde, The Picture of Dorian Gray

Chapter six
1. Information on Claude Shannon, information theory, and the space race received from the following sources: Information Theory, Aftab, Cheung, Kim, Thakkar, Yeddanapudi, retrieved from http://web.mit.edu/6.933/www/Fall2001/Shannon2.pdf. Retrieved on 31 July 2018;

https://en.wikipedia.org/wiki/Claude_Shannon;
https://en.wikipedia.org/wiki/Sputnik_crisis;
https://www.youtube.com/watch?v=5Be2YnlRl
g8, Google's story of send; Shannon, Claude
E. "The Bandwagon." IRE Transactions on
Information Theory. March 1956: 3; Dimitrov,
A. G., Lazar, A. A., & Victor, J. D. (2011).
Information theory in neuroscience. Journal of
computational neuroscience, 30(1), 1-5.

Chapter seven
1. First Theory. Milburn, J. Check email like a
minimalist. The Minimalists. Retrieved from
http://www.theminimalists.com/check/.
Retrieved on 28 July 2017.

2. Second Theory. Samuel, A. (2014) Limit the
time you spend on email. Harvard Business
Review. Retrieved from
https://hbr.org/2014/02/limit-the-time-you-
spend-on-email. Retrieved on 28 July 2017.

3. Purging emails. Seides, J. (2015) 6 ways to
cut the amount of time you spend on email.
Fast Company. Retrieved from
https://www.fastcompany.com/3043689/6-
ways-to-cut-the-amount-of-time-you-spend-
on-email. Retrieved on 28 July 2017.

4. Third theory. Firman, T. (2016). One CEO's
secret to checking email just once a day. Fast
Company. Retrieved from

https://www.fastcompany.com/3055967/one-ceos-secret-to-checking-email-just-once-a-day. Retrieved on 28 July 2017.

5. Fourth theory. Newport, C. (2016). A modest proposal: eliminate email. Retrieved from https://hbr.org/2016/02/a-modest-proposal-eliminate-email. Retrieved on 27 July 2017.

6. Fifth Theory. Dabbish, L. A., & Kraut, R. E. (2006, November). Email overload at work: an analysis of factors associated with email strain. In Proceedings of the 2006 20th anniversary conference on Computer supported cooperative work (pp. 431-440). ACM.

Epilogue

1. Strunk, W., & White, E. B. (1959). The Elements of Style/by William Strunk; with Revisions, an Introduction and a New Chapter on Writing by EB White. Macmillan.

------------------------This page was intentionally left blank------------------

Notes:

Notes:

_____

Notes:

_____

.

Email is simply information exchange between humans via digital
tools and technologies ~ be information wise ~
0427.04.03.2021.77.77.11035